THE JAMES BACKHOUSE LECTURES

This is one of a series of annual lectures which began in 1964 when Australia Yearly Meeting of the Religious Society of Friends was first established.

The lecture is named after James Backhouse, who travelled with his companion George Washington Walker throughout the Australian colonies from 1832 to 1838.

Backhouse and Walker were English Quakers who came to Australia with a particular concern for social justice. Having connections to social reform movements in the early colonies as well as in Britain, Backhouse and Walker planned to record their observations and make recommendations for positive change where needed.

Detailed observations were made of all the prisons and institutions visited by Backhouse and Walker. Their reports, submitted to local as well as British authorities, made recommendations for legislative reform. Many of the changes they initiated resulted in improvements to the health and wellbeing of convicts, Aboriginal people and the general population.

A naturalist and a botanist, James Backhouse is remembered also for his detailed accounts of native vegetation which were later published.

James Backhouse was welcomed by isolated communities and Friends throughout the colonies. He shared with all his concern for social justice and encouraged others in their faith. A number of Quaker meetings began as a result of his visit.

Australian Friends hope that these lectures, which reflect the experiences and ongoing concerns of Friends, may offer fresh insight and be a source of inspiration.

This particular lecture was delivered at Avondale College, New South Wales on 9th July 2018.

Jo Jordan
Presiding Clerk
July 2018

© The Religious Society of Friends (Quakers) in Australia, 2018

ISBN 9781921869686 (PB); ISBN 9781921869693 (eBook)

Produced by Australia Yearly Meeting of the Religious Society of Friends (Quakers) in Australia Incorporated
Download from www.quakersaustralia.info
or order/download from http://ipoz.biz/ipstore

THE JAMES BACKHOUSE LECTURES

2001 *Reconciling Opposites: Reflections on Peacemaking in South Africa*, Hendrik W van der Merwe

2002 *To Do Justly, and to Love Mercy: Learning from Quaker Service*, Mark Deasey

2003 *Respecting the Rights of Children and Young People: A New Perspective on Quaker Faith and Practice*, Helen Bayes

2004 *Growing Fruitful Friendship: A Garden Walk*, Ute Caspers

2005 *Peace is a Struggle*, David Johnson

2006 *One Heart and a Wrong Spirit: The Religious Society of Friends and Colonial Racism*, Polly O Walker

2007 *Support for Our True Selves: Nurturing the Space Where Leadings Flow*, Jenny Spinks

2008 *Faith, Hope and Doubt in Times of Uncertainty: Combining the Realms of Scientific and Spiritual Inquiry*, George Ellis

2009 *The Quaking Meeting: Transforming Our Selves, Our Meetings and the More-than-human World*, Helen Gould

2010 *Finding our voice: Our truth, community and journey as Australian Young Friends*, Australian Young Friends

2011 *A demanding and uncertain adventure: Exploration of a concern for Earth restoration and how we must live to pass on to our children*, Rosemary Morrow

2012 *From the inside out: Observations on Quaker work at the United Nations*, David Atwood

2013 *A Quaker astonomer reflects: Can a scientist also be religious?* Jocelyn Bell Burnell

2014 *'Our life is love, and peace, and tenderness': Bringing children into the centre of Quaker life and worship*, Tracy Bourne

2015 *'This we can do': Quaker faith in action through the Alternatives to Violence Project*, Sally Herzfeld & Alternatives to Violence Project Members

2016 *Everyday prophets*, Margery Post Abbott

2017 *Reflections on the 50th anniversary of the 1967 Referendum in the context of two Aboriginal life stories* by David Carline and Cheryl Buchanan

Front cover: *A symbol of the encounter between Taoism and Quakers* by Cho-Nyon Kim
Book design: David P. Reiter

2018
THE **JAMES BACKHOUSE** LECTURE

An Encounter between Quaker Mysticism and Taoism in Everyday Life

CHO-NYON KIM

Quakers
AUSTRALIA

Contents

About the author	vii
My Journey	1
My upbringing and the religiosity around me	4
Religious pluralism in Korea: Confucianism, Buddhism, Taoism and life (folk) faith	8
Encounters between Korean traditional religions and Christianity in Korea	12
The core idea of Taoism to be considered regarding Christianity or Quakerism	16
Ham Sok Hon's life and thought: Religious mysticism and everyday life	19
Ham Sok Hon's understanding of Christianity and other thought systems	25
My life as a Quaker	27
Bibliography	30

About the author

Cho-Nyon Kim is a Quaker from the Daejeon Quaker Meeting in South Korea. He is a professor of sociology. He edits a magazine on Ham Sok Hon, the prominent Korean Friend known internationally for his peace and justice witness. Cho-Nyon Kim is deeply committed to peace and care of the environment. His special interest is the encounter between Quaker mysticism and Taoism. He attended the World Gathering of Friends in Peru in January 2016 and the Australian Yearly Meeting of Friends in July 2016. He is an AVP–Korea facilitator. He will give the public lecture at the German Quaker Yearly Meeting in 2018.

My Journey

Everything changes repeatedly. Change is experienced in both the material and spiritual worlds. The meaning and the perspectives of the world, nations, states, religions and philosophies change all the time and in every situation. Sometimes, the changes are accompanied by a disappearance of content, while, at the same time, expanding to a new, abundant meaning. This phenomenon also occurs in religion. It is a matter of tradition and identity but also a matter of new enlightenment.

After I became acquainted with Quakers, I tried to discover the core of Quaker identity. This effort was a far cry from the Quaker tradition of not creating standards or creeds. However, after I was officially registered as a Quaker, I continued my search because I needed to know for myself what it is to be a Quaker. But the more I tried, the more abstract the Quakers' claim to live appeared. It was very frustrating.

The terms 'inner light', 'inner voice' and 'the person in me', which Quakers say, were hard to understand. They were as difficult to understand as the following concepts that I have heard since childhood from adults who have lived with Buddhism, Confucianism, Taoism, and Korea's own folk religions. For example, 'God', 'Holy Spirit', 'Messiah', 'Christ', 'Okhwangsangje', 'Yongwang', 'Yeomnadaewang', 'Geukrak', 'Seobangjeongto', 'Paradise' or 'Buddha in me' or 'Tao', 'Jinin, pure man', 'nature' or 'Buddha', which is said to be 'salvation' or 'liberation' (being Buddha) and so on—all were abstract. To my mind, nothing was obvious. However, it was clear that these abstract concepts were very closely related to everyday life, and I became more curious about Quakers' attitudes towards real life than any literal explanation or understanding of such concepts. What Quakers are very fond of and trying to accomplish are peace, simplicity, equality, community, truth, sustainability and integrity. It was very hard for me to understand them, and they were not easy to practise. I felt very deeply attracted to them, but when I tried to apply them to my life, they became very abstract. They are things that are relative and adaptable to the situation.

The world has become complicated. The community of life is broken, filled with confrontation and war rather than peace, and full of disagreement and division, increasing the differences rather than the togetherness. Where is the realisation of a life in the Quaker tradition, when the development and events of civilisation are increasing? In particular, how do we maintain the tradition of living a simple life in a modern civilisation that advocates a complex and superlative life?

I think the world has already progressed beyond the limits of sectarianism, considering the world as a whole, pursuing humanity over nation, country or region, and the fusion and coexistence of cultures. Quakers have been constantly trying to be rid of ties to a sect, and it is considered important to wear new clothes for a new age. According to the Oriental classics, the principle and life of Taoism valued the most peaceful, simple, general and ordinary things, and insisted on living a life based on nature beyond the form and norm. I think it would be meaningful to look into Taoism for the purpose of expanding the religiosity of Quakerism, not merely to compare them in a literal sense but to look at the spirituality and the mysticism of the covenant to supplement or expand Quakerism. This is because spirituality and mysticism are heard in the events we meet in our everyday lives.

In order to do that, I will first look at the general religious life in the Korean society that I was born into and grew up with. Then, I will briefly examine the evolution of Confucianism, Buddhism, folk religions, and the indigenous process of new Christianity, which have led Korean society for a long time. I am also going to examine what Quakerism pursues and discuss the key points that we pursue in Taoism.

Then I will look at the life and thought of Ham Sok Hon, one of Korea's early Quakers who lived in harmony with both Taoism and Quakerism. Finally, I would like to talk about the orientation of my life as a Quaker. These discussions, which will be organised in the form of questions, are not claims but expressions of wonder. This is a desire to re-establish Quakerism in myself. We see that Quakers are aging and the number of young Quakers is shrinking, so much so as to cause concern for the future of Quakerism. This may be a phenomenon that all religions are experiencing. However, many people look upon Quakerism as a religion for a new era, a religion that tries to find a new way and does not propagate and preach traditional Quakerism but secures an extended religiousness by combining the essence of one's own cultural and religious traditions with that of Quakerism. I feel this could be one of Quakers' ways of looking at a new era.

I am fortunate to have had the great pleasure of meeting Quakers. At the same time, I feel a great burden because a Quaker is considered an exemplar of realising faith in everyday life, and I want to put myself in that flow, but I am not in that life. I am very hesitant to tell someone that I am a Quaker, because I am not whole-heartedly true to that belief. Especially when I read the diary of the early Quaker, George Fox, I feel that I cannot experience such emotions as the trembling and the commitment to truth.

At that time, it seemed that the religious atmosphere that prevailed throughout society was much stronger than it is now. I feel that the society of the past as a whole had a much more religious atmosphere during the Reformation and expended greater efforts to adhere to the traditions of the established religions than now. At such a time, however, the lives of the early Quakers, such as George Fox, were very harsh, and they were treated strangely. It is very touching to learn that they lead a life following the faith and truth even in such circumstances.

It is like the impression I have when reading the Acts of the New Testament: I myself want to be living that life. I feel I am living in a very secular social atmosphere, an atmosphere of religion without religion. Of course, the number of people living their lives according to the systems and doctrines of religion is in fact very large, but the number of people practising a faithful religious life in formalised religion is very small. At the same time, the non-religious atmosphere seems to be the mainstream in the daily life of religion, politics, the economy, culture, scholarship and in social relations. It is not easy to live a deeply religious life at this time.

I have no experience of seeking the thorough truth that the early Friends had or of trying to realise that life. I have lived by a very ordinary and plain religion. Therefore, religion is very rare in my words, and it is difficult to find holiness in my everyday life. In fact, when I think about the question of whether I live according to the living word of Christ living in me, or the light in me, I am not confident about my answer. It is not easy to give a frank answer to the question of what Quaker life is today regardless of wearing a necklace with a cross on one's chest. However, I agreed to deliver this lecture because I had a desire to share my own concerns.

I want to ask how we can live a life that realises truth without distinction between religion and non-religion in a secular social atmosphere and cultural system. In asking that question, I will start with the following story—not the story of my Quaker enlightenment but of seeking a path to enlightenment.

My upbringing and the religiosity around me

I was born and raised in the non-religious tradition of a Confucian family. My family lived according to the education and life ethics of Confucian tradition. There were no characteristics of Buddhism or shamanism. Our family did not practise the tradition of shamanism, although many people in our village did. Our family never visited any Buddhist temples to meet Buddha, consult or pray for fortune. I never heard the word 'God' mentioned in family conversations. Instead, I heard that when a person dies, he or she is divided into a soul and a body, the soul is then carried to heaven, and the energy of the body is buried in the earth. I was very curious about this phenomenon. But I did not ask my grandparents serious questions about this, neither did my grandparents explain it. I merely grew up without asking and hence received no answer. According to the Confucian tradition, when a person dies, the descendants set up a house for the dead in the house. They prepare three meals a day for the dead to eat just as they would for living people. In the dead person's house, a soul box is built in which a braided thread of blue and red is kept. The braided thread symbolises the dead person's soul. The same was practised in my home, and it was the only religious act for our ancestors. Perhaps this should be the only religious act in our family. This was considered an act of filial piety: serving ancestral spirits. Confucianism, which has led Korean society and Korean family traditions, believed in the ethnocentric system as the ethic of life, and was exclusive to other religious activities.

There occurred, however, a problem in the family of my great-grandmother's older sons. Her daughter-in-law died early, and her great-grandson died. The great-grandmother became very sad. During that sad time, she met a Christian evangelist and heard the gospel of Christianity. From that time forward, she attended the church diligently and prayed sincerely. However, her method of prayer was the same as the traditional Korean family prayer system. She rose early in the morning, filled the pottery with clean water, washed her face with cold water and then gathered her hands together, rubbing them, and praying to God. It was a prayer for the dead young person and for the oldest living son for a good life. This style of prayer was common in society, consistent with the belief that a refreshed body at dawn enhances our prayers. Such tradition was passed on to her daughter-in-law and later to her granddaughter-in-law, but my grandfather was very displeased about Christianity coming into our family. There was an atmosphere of strange conflict between Confucian tradition and Christian faith. Of course, my great-grandmother and grandmother did not strictly follow a Christian tradition, so there was not too much trouble in my family in carrying out practices for Confucian family ethics. I grew up watching these situations, but I did not think about it and did not know how it related to my future or daily life.

There were no Buddhist temples in my home town and no Confucian shrines. My home-town villages were not where the ruling classes in Korean traditional society lived. Therefore, the villages did not live thoroughly in accordance with the Confucian ceremonies or the rules of Joseon dynastic society. At the end of the year or early in the new year, sacrifices for the peace of the village were made at a certain place. At the entrance to the village, a guardian deity had been constructed to guard the village. The ceremonies were also held there. Many people, depending on the season, prayed to their god according to their own family tradition—sometimes to the kitchen god, sometimes to the place of pottery, sometimes to the spring gods and sometimes to the tree gods. Strangely, large rocks, large trees or deep valleys or wells that were several hundred years old also became prayer centres and were worshipped—a practice that could be considered a kind of animism. In this way, God was present in their daily lives.

I thought there was a guard, or guardian of karma, that kept the house in any family. In Korean traditional society, there was no monotheistic concept as in Christianity. The gods were very diverse and numerous, each marked by the general public. There was a supreme god named Okhwangsangje, but it was a conceptual god, not an object of prayer in everyday life. Ancestor worship was very strong. On the anniversary of an ancestor's death, the people remembered him or her and held a memorial service. All these ceremonies and occasions used food as symbols—a consciousness that was consistent with beliefs. At that time, I assumed that the names of the gods were traditional, but they were individual, not part of an organised system. When people were sick or seriously ill, or when a family or person was experiencing a difficult time, they prayed earnestly to the gods they believed in. For most people, these prayers were religious ceremonies conducted as part of everyday life; they were not organised ceremonies.

When I was in high school, I went to the Christian church for the first time.

It was very strange. I sang hymns, prayed, read the Bible, listened to the sermon and received the pastor's blessing. I felt sincere, but a lot of doubt remained. I did not understand why the name of Jesus was used during prayer. I could not understand that Jesus died for me and that I would be saved if I believed in him, because he carried my sins on his shoulders. I was told that this was faith of the cross. How he could die in my place remained a puzzling question. I thought *I am me; he was him. How could he die for me? What does it mean to believe in him?*

In sermons, prayers, and hymns, I heard such words as blood, sin, original sin, death, salvation, resurrection, eternal life, destruction, hell, heaven, angel, devil, fight, victory, love, peace. Hymns that contained words of blood and sin seemed unintelligible and made me very nervous. Moreover, the contents of the hymns were so militant that I found it very uncomfortable to sing along together. How could love, curse and destruction coexist, and how could peace and war occur together? I found it very difficult to understand the original sin of Christianity. There was no such concept of original sin in Confucianism, Taoism or general folk beliefs.

The meaning of the faith was more difficult to understand. The education I had received since my childhood was Confucian ethics, which was based on the model of human goodness, righteousness, etiquette and wisdom. Confucian education stressed constant ethical self-improvement. Living without moral fault in everyday life was a very good virtue. Confucianism taught how to live harmoniously with the conflicts and contradictions in life. I had heard many controversial debates about whether the nature of humankind is good or evil, but I had never heard of original sin. According to the church, all human beings were born with original sin—a concept I could not understand. Although I heard the sermon, I could not comprehend that Jesus, who had lived in Palestine two thousand years ago, had shed his blood to liberate all people from original sin. As the son of God, he had no sin. If we believe that he came down to this earth to take away the sins of humanity and that he died for sinners, we will be saved from sin. How many people lived before Jesus, not hearing his name, and were therefore in a pit of destruction? I found that this required a leap of logic and was so difficult to believe. The dichotomy of heaven and hell evoked horror, but I could not take it seriously and thought it was the same thing as the Buddhist monastery's paradise. Of course, it seemed different from that of Buddhism, which means endless rebirth.

Another concept I failed to understand was that Jesus died for us. No one lives or dies for somebody else's life or death. When I said this to Christians, they answered that I did not have faith and that I should believe it unconditionally.

But how do you believe in incredible things? It was a revolving logic. When I read various theological writings, I could not understand their logic. Nevertheless, I continued to go to church and stayed in the system of Christianity. My Christian life has been a process of finding my own personality as a human being and the meaning of faith.

In the meantime, Howard H. Brinton's book *Friends for 300 Years* translated by Ham Sok Hon was introduced to Korea, and it opened my eyes. The form and contents evoked empathy; although, of course, it was not easy to understand at first. I also gained a little knowledge of Quakerism as I read another article by Ham Sok Hon. Occasionally, I attended Quaker meetings in Seoul and again during my stay in Germany. I arrived at the idea that when I returned to Korea I should become a Quaker, so my wife and I became members of the Northern Germany region. Of course, I did not consider the formality important at the time, but I did think about why I had to go through the formal process of Quaker membership. It would have been all right not to become a member and to continue worshipping with Friends in Germany, but I thought that when I returned to Korea, it would be strange for an attendee to host a Quaker meeting. Therefore, through interviews, I became an official member of the German Yearly Meeting.

I then returned to Korea and started studying Quakerism with some friends in Daejeon. We met every Sunday. The meeting started with one hour of silent worship and then ended with another hour of study. After six years of study meetings, we registered with FWCC[1] our aspiration to form a Quaker Monthly Meeting. We read religious scriptures in various ways: the New Testament and the Old Testament, Buddhist scriptures and Taoist scriptures, and occasionally Confucian classics. This led to a deeper understanding of the Quaker faith based on my Christianity, and to a broader degree of religiosity. As already mentioned, my background was in the traditions of Confucianism, Buddhism, Taoism and the folk beliefs of Korea. Although I have not studied them systematically, I feel that these traditions remain part of my life. Now, based on that, the life of Christianity and Quakerism directs me.

---

[1] Friends World Committee for Consultation.

Religious pluralism in Korea: Confucianism, Buddhism, Taoism and life (folk) faith

Historically, Korean society has been one of religious pluralism. Confucianism and Buddhism as national ruling ideologies have long dominated Korean society, and Taoism and folk religion as sources of life ethics have led people's everyday life in harmony with these foreign religions. In other words, although scholars' claims differ, one of Korea's traditional religions is Taoism and it came from China. However, it is true that Taoism is deeply rooted within Korean sentiments. Of course, unlike in China, the philosophical Taoism and religious Taoism have never been ideologies of any dynastic states in Korean history. However, in the days of Buddhism, which served as a national ideology for nearly one thousand years and—following Buddhism—Confucianism, these manifested in the faith and life of ordinary people.

Confucianism, a new dominant ideology, was introduced after the Buddhism that had flowed through China. These two ideologies have coexisted but in conflict politically and culturally. Sometimes, such religions have been persecuted, but they have never completely disappeared or perished. Therefore, when a dynasty changed or the social order could not be sustained by the existing ideology, new ideologies and religions evolved and brought new energy to society. When the ancient nations began to take root, people's faith did not have the capacity to lead national institutions or to assemble new intellectuals. What was needed at such a time was the power of a new religion. The influx of Buddhism into Korea coincided with the formation of the ancient state. Buddhism became the dominant ideology that led to the dynasties on the Korean Peninsula. However, at a later time, when exchanges took place between different societies and the international community, new religions and ideologies were required and Confucianism was adopted.

Confucianism served as a strong ruling ideology of the Joseon Dynasty. However, the overly stringent Confucian system imposed very strict limitations on daily life, the economy and political life as well as the spiritual world. At that time, new religions and philosophies were introduced through China. Catholicism came in the latter half of the eighteenth century. For those who had received inhumane treatment because of the Confucian ethics of a rigid class system, the idea of Christian equality held great appeal. Catholicism played a very large role in awakening sleeping souls. The news that all humans are equal before God became the gospel. However, such thoughts and beliefs were perceived by the ruling class as a crisis that could destroy the existing order. At that time, elite groups who were inclined to reform or who could not directly participate in real politics became more interested in these new ideas and soon adopted the new religious ideology to improve the lives of ordinary citizens. The ruling class then began to severely persecute Christians. The controversy over ancestor worship in China also happened in Korea.

A hundred years later, Protestantism was introduced to Korea. The Catholics were very much opposed to Confucianism, and persecuted many. However, the Protestants who came after the Catholics had no difficulty with Confucian ideology. Protestantism, which brought medical science, education, the natural sciences and technology, drew interest from many ordinary people, dynasties and ruling elites, especially as the dynasty lost power and the forced integration and reign of Japan began. At that time, the national consciousness and Protestantism of the Korean people coincided due to the loss of national rights. As Protestants entered, Korea opened its doors to America and Europe and became interested in Western science, democracy and education. These things grew with nationalism, and the Protestant mission strategy was successful in its appeal to Koreans. Christian ideas were considerably different from the Confucian and Buddhist lifestyles that had dominated Korea. At that time, there was a movement to form a new type of religion by rearranging the religious systems in Korean society and history, but that movement was not successful.

However, a new religious movement, Donghak (the Eastern learning), which incorporated Korean traditional ideas, Christian gods and human thoughts, appealed to civilian society. Subsequently, it was thoroughly persecuted by the forces that led politics among the ruling classes because the core of Donghak ideology was very different from what was claimed in Confucianism and Buddhism. Although persecuted, Donghak spread widely, and it soon became deeply embedded. When protesting Japanese rule, Donghak cooperated with

Protestantism over the issue of national independence, but it was prohibited from public activities by the Japanese government and lost influence because of systematic persecution.

Eventually, Buddhism, Confucianism, traditional religion and Christianity all became part of Korean society and played important roles in mental activities and everyday life. Whenever a new religion or thought system comes into existence, conflicts with existing religions or ideological systems arise; however, over time, the new ideologies compromise or even merge with the traditional spiritual worlds, thought systems and lifestyles. That is to say, the new Confucianism absorbed Buddhism, and Buddhism could not help but absorb the new Confucianism. At the same time, Christianity had to accept the ideologies and lifestyles of Buddhism and Confucianism, which were deeply rooted in the land. In logic and doctrine, many things were absorbed by the other, but in practice in everyday life, people had to mix with and tolerate each other. In other words, the existing ideological system partially accepted the new thought system and thus improved its own, and the new thought system had to incorporate or inculcate existing ideas or settle, becoming a reality that enabled both conflict and coexistence. The realisation that some of the core ideas in other religions and thought systems may be different but could be accepted led to the opposite of conflict and coexistence. In order to establish and maintain one's own religion or thought system, one has to argue that it is different from others, but at the same time one has no other choice but to utilise or borrow key elements from others. It represents the contradiction and dilemma of religion in daily life, a clear indication that in a multi-religious society, such as Korea, one's own religion is negotiated with other religions. It demonstrates that a religion adheres to its immaculacy while at the same time accepting and evolving others. At this point, radical believers claim that 'all religions are one'. In other words, religious pluralism is encountered in religious unity. All religions start in their own way in their own places but meet in the ultimate. In this respect, the pluralism of religion is asserted and acknowledged in Korean society, and behind it, all religions reach one religion. This makes it possible for the evolution of religion—that is, for religions to converse and meet with other religions.

Korean preoccupations with religion, ideology and everyday life are very similar to those in China because they came from China or through China. For example, Confucianism and Taoism arrived from China, and Buddhism and Catholicism arrived through China. They had already evolved to a great extent or arrived after undergoing conflicts during enculturation and missions. Protestantism arrived in Korea partly through China but mainly via American and Western missionaries. The early arrivals converged in conflict with folk religions; the later arrivals reconciled with the foreign and folk religions that preceded them. The mainstream religions that exist now are Confucianism, Buddhism, Taoism and Christianity. They have combined with unique folk religions and other foreign religions and have become Koreanised. From my early childhood, I grew up in the spiritual form of wisdom, experience, scholarship, morality and religion, mixed with Confucianism, Taoism, Buddhism and folk beliefs through the stories of old men, ancestors, or life story. I grew up in a living culture where various religions melded through stories and ordinary life, not through systematic education or religious activities. Therefore, before I met Christianity, the old religious traditions of Korean society had already flowed into me. Before the ancient state was formed, there were many claims that it should accept and spread the ideas of folk religion, Confucianism, Buddhism and Taoism in order to create a spiritual foundation for the state. Even though there were some conflicts with other ideas following the formation of the state and the dominant ideology, I think that the result was predominately a mutually tolerant atmosphere.

Encounters between Korean traditional religions and Christianity in Korea

No matter which religion it is, if it is to spread its roots in new places, it cannot insist on retaining its original contents. The fact that a religion has roots in a particular place means that it has settled in the culture through a long historical process. One cannot ignore the attitudes, the thoughts and the rituals of life that have been resident in the area up to that time. New religions must also enter the language (concepts) used. Here, the newly preached religions change their original form, and on the side that accepts them, face very serious conflicts. Sometimes, it appears to be a question of dialogue, sometimes an aspect of persecution, sometimes indifference. The preaching of a new religion must be related to what has already taken place in the land. Religions evolve via these processes.

As I mentioned, Korea is a multi-religious society. Over the course of history, many religions at different times became the dominant ideology of the nation and led the life culture. Even when a new religion became the dominant ideology, past religions and cultures that were pushed to one side did not disappear completely, but remained functioning in life, mind, system and consciousness. They survived in the new regime and spread to new areas because there were some points of contact between them. A point of contact opens up the possibility of coexistence and of dialogue and religious enculturation that can create a kind of universal human society. Human beings have always had a common religiosity, no matter where they live. This is the basis for the coexistence of different religions, and all religions evolve, influenced by different religions.

From this position, there is a need to compare Christianity with the many religions that have existed in Korea, although it is impossible and meaningless to compare Christianity with them directly. The languages, concepts and images used are constantly changing, and names differ for the same deity, but even in those religions that use the same name, images change according to the time and situation. They may be referred to as gods, heaven, Tao or absolute, but they are the same in that they are ultimate beings—the first, the last, the greatest, the deepest—and they exist within the individual. They have been used as objects of faith, though the terms and images used differed in practice. Also the same was the effort to escape from sin, to go beyond pain and into the world of liberation and to try to move from restraint to a free state. Therefore, it would be meaningful to look briefly at the differences and commonalities in faith and practice.

As mentioned, Buddhism entered the Korean Peninsula through China. Of course, in China, Buddhism had undergone many changes and been altered in coexistence and in controversy with new religions, but in the Korean Peninsula, each religion has undergone another process of refraction or change. That is why we use the same name, but the content is very different.

Confucianism does not speak of sin. Of course, Confucianism petitions to heaven, begs to the gods, prays, but it does not do so for liberation from sin but for the wellbeing of the nation and the human race and for solutions to temporal problems. So, regarding what humans and groups do, the key is to recognise the will of heaven and live that way. Constant self-discipline is necessary to follow the will of the heavens and is the most important thing in life. One way was to worship the ancestors by doing good things. At this point, Confucianism caused great conflict with Christianity. The worship of ancestors was not a religious act but a ritual of family tradition. This problem caused trouble in all kinds of family events and was a big issue in China and Korea. The conflict with the Catholic Church on this issue has now been resolved but remains a problem with Protestantism. Christians, of course, have deep thoughts about their ancestors, but they have considerable flexibility in the matter of rituals. It can be a kind of compromise. There are no big problems with regard to other social and ethical issues.

Regarding relations between folk religion and Christianity, Shamanism, described as 'no religion' or 'folk religion', spread widely in Korean society as a daily life faith rather than as a religion in the Western style. There was a great god named Okhwangsangje, but he was not the object of prayer. Rather, the gods that were subject to prayer varied greatly depending on the region, race, family and age. There was no hierarchy among the various gods; they simply functioned in daily life. Folk religion was based on the ceremony and life of Confucianism, Buddhism and Christianity. In this sense, folk religion—that is, shamanistic folk religion—must be said to be the present religion that continues to be created. It should be seen that it is deeply rooted in the daily life and emotion of Koreans.

Nowadays, Confucianism functions only as a life ethic; it does not exist as religious education or in any form of systematic organisation. There are no temples, schools or authoritative Confucian teachers. It is very common in Western countries to say that Korea is a Confucian society, but it is unclear whether the claim is justifiable, because a long traditional culture remained. Confucianism emphasises ethics that regulate human and social relations and underpin daily life. It is a meaningful evaluation to call Korea a Confucian society, in the sense that Koreans live a life in keeping with traditional Confucianism rather than studying the doctrine deeply and revering it. In spite of this, Koreans assume that human beings are able to reach perfection through debating whether the intrinsic nature of human beings is good (Mencius school) or evil (Xunzi school). So, they pursue self-discipline constantly, and they accept that it is very natural to continue to pursue self-growth and self-reflection even though they also accept the doctrine of Christian salvation through faith in Jesus.

Buddhism has many temples, and there are many schools training Buddhist monks. It is true that today there are fewer students than in the past, and fewer aspiring Buddhists, but in general, Buddhist beliefs have not been reduced significantly. There are universities and high schools operated by Buddhist societies, and many institutions provide Buddhist funeral services. Buddhism plays a large role in comforting the dead, finding the way to paradise and comforting the survivors. It operates various programs for those needing to find calm and to meet peace. The message that everyone possesses Buddha-nature and can attain Buddhahood gives immense hope to ordinary people. Some Buddhist scholars claim they can reach enlightenment or that they can reach certain levels by studying and training more and more. Whatever they claim, they have something in common. The position of Mahayana Buddhism—which acknowledges that there is absolute in the relative; nirvana in many things, such as the forest; and sacredness in the mundane world—is strong in Korean Buddhism. The difference between the Buddhist sects is not so large, but the union between Buddhism and the folk religions is unusual. This would be the result of the spread of Buddhism and its adaptation to Korean society. In addition, the ceremony of ancestor worship has continued in Buddhism. The concept of nirvana and liberation would have been a factor in the non-confrontational acceptance of Christianity and its concepts of salvation and heaven.

Taoism is not a dominant ideology in Korea. There are no shrines, teachers or structured organisation. According to Taoist philosophy, one must live a life of complete simplicity and honesty in harmony with nature. This may be possible for those Koreans who have retired from the workforce or who have withdrawn from social life. But living in harmony with nature would be difficult for most contemporary Koreans. Taoist philosophy is especially critical about civilisation. When Koreans experience the restlessness and the meaninglessness of their constantly changing society, the contemplation that is emphasised in Taoism can give them new energy.

In Korea, there are many Christian educational institutions: elementary schools, middle schools, high schools and universities, and there are theological educational institutions that train Christian leaders. In addition, there are Christian-run hospitals and various social service agencies to assist society as a whole, especially those experiencing hardship. Participation in politics and business circles by Christian Koreans is particularly encouraged in new movements. Progressive Christianity expresses interest in other religions, but conservative Christianity is more interested in conversion and mission. Religious conflicts are deepening within conservative Christian sects.

Among the intellectuals who devote themselves to each religion, those who think about enculturation have much interaction with each other. Ecumenical Christians also interact with clerics and followers of other religions. Among them, there is little controversy regarding the premise of conversion, but there are many concerns about how to accept and recognise the doctrines and ethics of other religions and apply them to everyday life. Religious proponents of either liberal or conservative tendencies tend to cooperate with one another on the issues that each is interested in. However, it is not easy for liberalists and conservatives to interact within the same religion. Instead, it is those with the same tendencies but who practise different religions that tend to interact on the problems to be solved.

The core idea of Taoism to be considered regarding Christianity or Quakerism

Tao, the ultimate reality in Taoism, cannot be adequately expressed in finite human thought, studies, languages and feelings. Everything that comes out of the ultimate reality is infinitely mysterious and delicate. There is no shape, no image; therefore, it is not subject to objective recognition and cannot be recognised as rational thought or reasoning. It is only talked about as a symbol, and because the name and reality do not coincide at the moment of naming, in the end it is a reality that needs to be recognised, experienced and felt through denial. In other words, because everything that humans have is unrecognised, they must reject all that they have in order to enter the world of the Tao.

In particular, silence in Quaker life and the silent prayer in unprogrammed Quaker worship could reference the Zen meditation of Buddhism. Zen meditation is a method of purifying the corrupted human mind. Its purpose is to realise the ultimate truth by first emptying the mind. One must abandon all obsessions and enter into the state of mindlessness. In this way, one realises the truth of nothingness as the ultimate reality beyond all relative things and can reach the level of liberation, which meets the Buddha through the intuition of the inner mind. This can be said to correspond with the prayers of Christian practitioners who empty their minds and open themselves to God alone, and it is consistent with the worship of a Quaker who, in the midst of calmness, seeks and waits for the promptings of God. In other words, encounter through self-denial. The Taoist objective of reaching absolute affirmation through rejection is compatible with Quaker thought.

At this point, it would be meaningful to briefly review the concept of Taoism in three parts: practising social ethics, simplicity and Tao. What confidence and comfort do ordinary people gain when reading *Tao Te Ching*? This does not mean that one can advance from reading *Tao Te Ching* to the highest level of Taoism; there is no fixed point that a person must reach, but each needs to perceive the truthful process to the best of their ability. It is not possible to set the same standard for young children, young adults and the elderly. Each individual has different criteria and different standards. This is the new possibility of the Taoist philosophy.

The mystic experience of Taoism is not fascinating but dark, neutral and uncertain. It is not based on faith but on the direct experience of God and is a mystery that naturally occurs when living a simple life. I think of the Taoist philosophy as divided into principles, dynamic forces, actions or practices of life.

First, I wish to consider an understanding of Tao (Ô³). Tao is transcendent and intrinsic as absolute reality. Everything has evolved from it. Therefore, it is the mother of all, a loving and productive reality. However, as a being of nothingness, its image cannot be drawn. Non-existence is explained only by negation and cannot be heard, seen, caught or named. It can only be seen and explained as a result of action. The source of life is black darkness, and black chaos in that sense, but Tao gives the possibility of infinity. Tao can be described as deep valleys that are empty but accommodate everything: the lowest and deepest sea, the mother, or the water that flows only to the lowlands. Here, it embodies the characteristics of revelation and salvation, the concept of eternal life. It is said that salvation and eternal life are created by oneself. Tao is not exclusive to any particular class but is directly connected to all people's lives. The appearance and realisation of Tao cannot be expressed in words but is always ordinary: a kind of Logos and a way. Like a road, Tao shows the way, containing both sides of principle, relativity and equality that apply to real life. The work of balancing maintains absolute equality beyond the use of the opposing world, so there is no preciousness, no inferiority, no high and low, and no fast and slow.

The way in which Tao works, or the way in which people live in accordance with Tao, is 'doing nothing' (無爲). Interpreted literally, this means 'not doing anything'. However, when considering the whole context and flow, a different, contradictory interpretation emerges, which is to do everything by *not* doing. It is said to be as natural as the water overflowing from a bowl or a pond when it is full. The water flows downwards when tilted, the young sprout shoots in warm spring weather, the temperature gradually lowers when heat reaches the maximum and rises as it approaches the minimum. Likewise, Tao does not work by human power but proceeds in its own way and time. This means that we should not regulate or direct life by civilisation and institution. 'Doing nothing' is the pursuit of a life that renounces morality, law and form. An anarchistic life can be considered. So, being soft, compassionate, humble and weak can be said to be elements of inexperience. In this way, there is a possibility that the social aspects of contention and violence can be overcome. Should this term 'positive passivity' be considered contradictory?

This kind of life is possible only by returning to 'natural disposition' (the simplest and primitive state, p'o ÚÔ). The state of natural disposition is simple but not easily explained. It is like a blank slate, infant-like, a return to the roots. So, Lao-tze insists that the five colours blind the eyes, the five sounds darken the ears, and the five flavours defile the mouth. In other words, these embellishments send the human mind mad, lead to a life full of covetousness and mark the beginning of an unethical civilisation. Taoism wants 'natural disposition'—that is, always rustic, not polished, a life in which man pursues freedom. It is the attitude and life of the Ssial (씨알; seed) as claimed by Ham Sok Hon. So, how did Ham Sok Hon incorporate this Taoism thought system into his life by combining it with the Christian system?

Ham Sok Hon's life and thought: Religious mysticism and everyday life

It is necessary to take a brief look at the religious thought and life of Ham Sok Hon, an early Korean Quaker and a modern philosopher (thinker). He first encountered Christianity in his youth and lived the rest of his life as a Christian. But his life journey varied a great deal. He started out as a Presbyterian and grew up within this denomination. When he was studying in Japan, he learned a 'non-Church faith movement' from Uchimura Kanjo and lived this way for a considerable period. He became a Quaker when he reached a mature age. Korean Quakers are influenced by Ham Sok Hon, and I believe that I was also much influenced by him.

Ham Sok Hon read many of Rabindranath Tagore's books. He also read Gandhi, Tolstoy, Ruskin, Carlyle, Schweitzer and H. G. Wells. Of course, he also read books on communism. During the Korean War, he read the *Bhagavad-Gita* and studied Indian thought. Through reading, he realised there was no fundamental difference between Christianity and Buddhism, and he came to the conclusion that all religions are one. When he began to read Chuang-tze, he felt his shell cracking off, bit by bit. He thought deeply about the historical Jesus, eternal life, heaven, salvation and so on. He declared:

> The idea of being a heretic or an authentic is an old idea. Where is the road in the air? Go endlessly; endlessly climb up the road. As long as you are a relative being, you are going to go your way, which is just one of infinite ways. I am only going to go my way. I am not qualified to define it. There is no heresy. Only those who claim to be heresy are heresy.

Following this declaration, Ham Sok Hon walked his own faith path. Through this declaration, he was able to divorce himself from the union church and go his own way: 'So I am not alone in my father's bosom, and I have seen so many ways to climb the mountain of truth.' Anyone can say that his or her way is the only way, but this is only subjective. There are as many ways to climb as there are people; although, in an absolute place, one road is the only way. It is religion in a relative world, and no religion is unique—just one of many religions. The thought that Christianity is the only true religion is a narrow idea in the relative system. So, all religions should be humble. Individual religions are not large enough to hold God. So, Ham Sok Hon, as much as possible, tried to live by the spirit of freedom, without holding onto the 'formality' that began with a symbol.

To him, the true path is the way that either you or I, or a Christian or a pagan, walk together. 'I am not the only son. So, now you have to sacrifice your self-creed'. 'To know whether it is authentic or superstition is possible only between God and me'). 'I believe not only for myself but for others, finally, the world must be saved. Belief in faith for future generations is a truly saving faith. It [truth] is in all past mankind and is the future humanity. In this way, no one will perish'.

Ham Sok Hon waits for a new religion to appear, regarding present religions as old beliefs that do not fit into the new age. The reasons for this are:

1. The completion of Christian doctrine
2. Increasingly institutionalising
3. Being defensive, not being offensive
4. Increasingly antagonistic
5. Strong internal conflict

These reasons are why a new religion is needed. An old religion predicts and orders a new one in the same way as rot stimulates or severe shock results in a new flow. There are some signs that the time when a new religion will be born is not far away:

1. The totally different nature of modern war
2. The progress in atomic science
3. Worldview issues
4. The development of biotechnology
5. The whole world connected as a single network

What will the new religion be like? New religions come from the waiting mind. It will appear in the following way.

1. 'If you say the shape of the face is round, it means one. [...] Religion which refuses this belief (all religions are one) will fall in the future. [...] He will give you a Word to make the whole world one house. [...] In the future, the world will be one, and there will be one religion.'

2. 'The religion would be a colourless face. It means that it must become more rational. [...] The reasoning belongs to the realm of science. [...] Science and religion are all growing aspects of life, but each has depreciated the other by criticising. [...] Those who are trapped in the emotions of winning and losing cannot go to heaven. Neither science nor religion wins. It is not a religion or a science until one enters the world of eternal infinity.'

3. 'This is a matter of humanity. It is a matter of how people think about themselves. [...] What to do about God, what to do about the natural world? These questions reflect a person's view of himself. [...] Future religions should be religions that re-create this tired life, so they must have a new human perspective to reunite the divided person. Body would not interfere with soul, and soul would not exclude body'. 'It is the religion of mind because it is one of personality and logic, and it is the religion of enlightenment because it is one of mind. [...] It always lives here and now. "Here and now" is the reality. 'Religion does not forget reality but saves reality. It requires the least amount of organisation to deliver reality'. 'It is not a giant organisation, but a minimal organisation and form. The religion of the future is the religion of the here and now. Therefore, without thinking of the here and now, there can be no salvation and no repentance. It's only nonsense […] Of course, the purpose is heaven. It is the way of religion to ascend to heaven. But there are no birds that fly without encountering land. The Word, "It is done in the earth, as it is in heaven," means to consider the importance of tense'

4. Authentic religion regards the people's aliveness as important. 'Religion really does not make the people into an [sic] hallucination and sleep but wakes them up and fights them. [...] As long as no one can fight evil and become a good spirit,

we cannot close our eyes to reality. Sin is a reality, reality is a sinful being, and sin is a social phenomenon, so that living religion is a systematic activity of those who are determined to fight against evil. [...] God, who is the winner of the fighting against the sin of reality, is Christ. Our religion must be realistic and scientific .' How, then, will we fight against the reality?

5. There are two goals to fight. 'God and the people, these two are one. If God is the head, his feet are in the people. That the feet of the holy God take steps on and are covered with dust, is just the people. [...] God's service is in the service of the people. The highest is at the lowest, the most holy is at the most vulgar, and the largest is at the smallest. Truth is in the people. The concept that the people are the feet of God means that the people are the reflection of the all visible. [...] Washing feet is washing the people. An absolute and holy God has no problem with cleaning the feet of those who are dirty. So, Christ said, "What you do to one of the least of my brothers is what you do to me." The extremely small is the people. The meaning of small is low. There is nothing greater than the low on earth, though it is unbelievably low compared in the heaven. A church, a nation, a culture, and a world can be said to be nothing more than architecture built on the surface.' An extremely small organisation is needed to wake up the people, the Ssial (seed). In this way, Ham Sok Hon was already a Quaker before he met other Quakers. When they met each other, it was merely a confirmation that their beliefs were the same.

Ham Sok Hon's argument can be summarised as follows: He is freed from the idea that Christianity is the only religion and that the Bible alone proclaims complete truth. He is convinced that the world must be one, encompassing science and globalisation. Therefore, he is sure that nationalism must be overcome, and all religions represent the Word of God. He believes it is important to have one's own religion. The world's salvation is represented by the individual's trials. To have 'a religion of one's own' requires a believer to come face-to-face with God, without a mediator, to confront God individually—not in the manner of a religion with many followers. 'Christ does not represent anyone. He is the person who stands right in front of God, that is Christ.' So, Ham Sok Hon wants to stand before God as a Christian. At the same time, he liked to read Lao-tze and Chuang-tze. He also liked Gandhi, who said, 'If there is a truth valuable to sacrifice one's life, that is, every human being must live together.' At the same time, Ham Sok Hon became an absolute positivist influenced by Carlyle, who said, 'Eternal affirmation, which is ultimate affirmation, is reached through the ultimate negation of everything.' He loves the freedom that God has given, so he becomes a free man. What do we do with such liberty? The free individual is not an admiral but an individual who represents the whole. Therefore, the fusion of such individuals and the whole is important. God, manifested in the reality, represents the whole as a flow in the personal life.

One is 'to realise that you should share your neighbour with yourselves, to serve your God with all your heart and all your soul and to serve your neighbour as yourself'. The individual and the whole are not separate to Ham Sok Hon. You are in me, I am in you. I am the whole within you. Therefore, Ham Sok Hon sees the spiritual community as a new religion that frees the individual while focusing on the individual as a whole. He experiences this in Quakerism.

As a Quaker, he cannot condone violence, so is committed to opposing war. In this way, he believes the pacifist element of Quakerism is closest to Eastern thought. Ham Sok Hon has always been interested in the thought of Lao-tze and Chuang-tze and the Zen of Buddhism, and he used this substantially in everyday life.

Ham Sok Hon believed that after the end of World War II the social life of human beings would be greatly changed. He thought that the way of life and the social structure itself would become fundamentally different, not merely to the extent that the boundaries would be changed. How would it differ? What would the role of religion be? Would religion try to stand in the way of a new civilisation? He saw that existing religions would not endure, because they were closely connected with politics. World War II had seen the birth of the superpower, nationalism and continued domination. Therefore, he thought that a new vision of nationhood should be established. He claimed that a country must be for the people, and the notion that the people should exist for the nation should be abolished. If this were to be the case, it would need to be understood in terms of Eastern thought.

He saw salvation in Christianity and nirvana in Buddhism as simply different names for the same concept. For example, human thought and behaviour remain the same whether expressed as 'sin' in Christianity or as 'ignorance' in Buddhism. In this way, there is nothing to cause conflict between the two religions. The place that Lao-tze and Chuang-tze call 'Tao', is the place of God that Christians seek. If we do not analyse these concepts ideologically but instead see them through the mind of a believer, the place is the same.

One thing is clear: We do not aspire to the afterlife as a luxurious life forever lived as an extension of today's world (3, 160). Through meditation and prayer, one is emptied and the other is filled by the absorption of truth. In this, Christianity and Zen converge.

Ham Sok Hon did not wish to distinguish between the plural, the whole, the one; between the East and the West; or between Christianity, Buddhism, Zen and Taoism. Rather, he believed that ideas may be shared so that everything is one. All are children of God. Would this new religion be perfect? It was not about perfection. For Ham Sok Hon, religion is never complete but continues to change, flow and grow. The process of religion, the faith on the path, is the only thing that grows. It is a living religion that can follow the path. In reality, to those who think of God as unfinished and growing, religion and faith can never be complete and manifest.

Ham Sok Hon's understanding of Christianity and other thought systems

It is very important to grasp the relationship between Eastern philosophy and Ham Sok Hon's understanding of Jesus. The idea of the Ssial (씨앗), which he created in the last years of his life, refers to the 'pure man'. A good example of the pure man is Jesus. 'No one can enter the kingdom of heaven unless he is like a child.' To Jesus, a child represents purity. The way to achieve this is to be born again, to return to one's original innocent self. Eastern thought is the same. Taoists, especially, think deeply about the child's mind. He who becomes as a child is a person with a very deep virtue.

Let us look at Lao-tze, Chapter 28. If you know the male (heaven, Yang) and defend the female (land, Yin), you will receive the water of the valley, the water of life under the earth. Then you will return to the child's heart without losing the purest virtue of nature. If you take advantage of virtue, you become like an infant. Bees or insects do not sting, nor birds and ducks peck. This is a simple and pure man that Lao-tze sees.

Did Ham Sok Hon regard Ssial in this way? Ssial may be soft like a child's hand but is hard to hold and can be regarded as weak even though everything is arranged around it. Therefore, the childlike mind is the true heart, the heart as it was in the beginning. If you lose the true heart, you lose Ssial. Isn't this the heart of Ssial? Ham Sok Hon seems to have regarded the true person practising Christianity or the philosophy of Lao-tze as the heart of Ssial. Let's look in depth at how he comprehended the thoughts of Lao-tze and Chuang-tze.

Ham Sok Hon interpreted the thoughts of Lao-tze and Chuang-tze, in the following way. The intention of Lao-tze and Chuang-tze was to live beyond the phenomenon of reality. This is not to say that to transcend means to discard. This phenomenon is not a dream, nor a falsity, nor an evil that should be discarded, as some people believe. Lao-tze and Chuang-tze did not think so and did not live that way either. We are born into the world of reality: we have no choice, nor can we avoid it. It is a natural thing and inevitable because it is nature. We cannot help that. Man is a thinking being, so our attitudes are what matters. We can understand, judge good and bad, choose or forsake. 'A complicated problem arises between the thinking me and the world that surrounds me and those who think like me.'

'I know that the relative emerged from the absolute by seeing the relative apart from the absolute. That is transcending reality. 'Absolute' is infinite eternity and 'relative' is also eternal infinity. It is called "a mystery within a mystery" because it becomes one by the absolute in the relative. It is also called "the gate of all subtleties". The lives of Lao-tze and Chuang-tze begin at Tao and end at Tao. The end is the beginning, the beginning the end.'

Tao is causeless because it is the basis of everything. It is said that it is nature itself, and it is said to be nothing. 'What can be done to achieve the way (Tao)?' Lao-tze emphasises futility, silence and unselfishness in one's thinking, and doing nothing, weakness, non-violence and restoration in one's practice. Ham Sok Hon therefore acknowledged Lao-tze as a pacifist. 'No one has ever cried purely for pacifism.' Moreover, this was during the time of the Chunchu States, which emphasised national prosperity and military power. Lao-tze emphasised doing nothing rather than becoming political. This applies to the principle of all life—that is to say, all belief in life and the ability to self-govern.

As poor as Chuang-tze was, he disliked the prospect of a government post and said he preferred to be as the pigs herded into the gutter rather than live in a house designed for extravagant ceremony. He related this philosophy to the messenger who had been sent by the king to offer Chuang-tze a high post in the government. Instead of adopting such a high position, Chuang-tze remained an ordinary person but with a fiery determination to rescue Ssial, who lived a life of exploitation under a tyrannical ruler. This standing is linked to the life of Jesus. Ham Sok Hon expressed this position on life in his famous article 'The Spirit of Wilderness'. This spirit is seen in the life of prophets such as Isaiah, Jeremiah and Amos in the Old Testament. Ham Sok Hon's critique of nationalism is obviously derived from the unregulated politics of Lao-tze and Chuang-tze and from the concept of the heavenly kingdom of Jesus. It is the fusion of these ideas that foretells a new world of truth and a nation that does not ignore or forsake the real world. Is this also the Quaker spirit?

My life as a Quaker

Am I able to practice Quakerism in my daily life? Am I able to keep that tradition, as a Quaker who sees faith and practice as either equally important or as one? When I think about it, I have grave doubts. In today's highly civilised society, I have to live in luxury compared with ancient times, so what is humble and simple living? How can I live without destroying the nature's ecosystem when I am aware that birth itself is an environmental destruction? In what way can we live together peacefully when the pattern of life leads to competition and strife from beginning to end? In an overly systemised and organised society, is it possible to live under soul guidance like a natural and windy spirit? Strangely, in a modern society becoming increasingly nationalistic, how can I practise the beliefs and philosophy that humankind belongs to one life system? How can I follow the Quaker tradition of not swearing oaths or pledges in a digitalised modern world where almost everything is full of such things? When I think about this, my breath seems to be stifled. But I feel that finding a little road to life in the frustrating and obstructed reality is essential for a Quaker. Isn't it a mystery to experience in everyday life, or in a life awaiting revelation, a need for a practical narrow path that captures a feeling from an invisible reality? So, it is time to wait for a mystic experience in a life that has no mystery.

I want to lead my life in the following way, at least. There is one hope and one reality on the Korean Peninsula. In other words, there is an ideology that the nation should form one country, but the reality is that it is divided into two countries, which fight each other. My philosophy and belief are that the entire human race must transcend nations and countries. I think that we should pay close attention to how we can create a society that lives peacefully when all nations are becoming more self-centred. In order to do that, it is my job to first make myself peaceful and to live with a peaceful mind. At the same time, it is necessary to share a peaceful life with the people around me. To that end, I try to practise keeping a smile on my face and in my mind. I must endeavour to acknowledge and tolerate others, but I should also challenge the tradition and social trend of making everything uniform. I am trying to launch a campaign that no war should take place on the Korean Peninsula. Also, I am trying to initiate a peace pilgrimage and introduce the energy of peace into places of severe conflict, particularly with the elderly who think there should be no more war on the Korean Peninsula, no matter whether they are on the left or on the right. Given that the threat of a nuclear war between the United States and North Korea is on the rise, pilgrimage activities for peace are very important now, I think. We are all different, but at the same time, we are one. So, we are friends. I want to undertake a peace pilgrimage to realise this.

Peace energy senses the need to train individuals creatively to change their violent tendencies into a state of non-violence and peace. This was the result of my experience and participation as an activist for the Alternatives to Violence Project (AVP). We should practise non-violence in our personal lives and our relationships with others, believe that one can acknowledge and respect oneself, respect and care for others, solve all problems in a non-violent way, think deeply before acting and expect the best result. I was convinced of these things when taking part in several workshops with AVP. Therefore, I consider trying to live in this way as my important life task. Of course, there is no order, but I hope that I can contribute to the peace of society through training myself to be peaceful.

I want to spread the message of peace to ordinary citizens through research on non-violent thoughts, lectures and forums. In daily life, I wish to assist others to love their enemy, bless those who are different and trust those who have no truth. In this way, the Taoist philosophy that softness encompasses strength and that softness dissolves rigidity can become a habit incorporated into daily life. This training begins with the belief that all people have the possibility to enter such a state. It also encompasses a common belief that all people have an inner light, that there is an inner teacher, and that all can find a way to Buddha-nature and get in touch with Tao. This is the mystical experience of everyday life. Mysticism is a very normal life.

However, in contemporary civilised society, Koreans especially, lack sufficient daily rest and do not practise deep breathing. Therefore, there are many people who are not always burdened themselves, decide not to live their own lives, and yet are struggling with external pressures and mood. As one philosopher has said, modern society is an exhausted society. I do not have the ability and vision to lead to a place of peace those who feel tired, but I want to create an atmosphere where I can talk with them as a friend. Of course, I am not a professional counsellor, nor a conflict solver, nor a person who has trained others. But I want to be a friend to troubled people who cannot establish themselves or who are conflicted. I feel that this is a way to live with the truth in my own heart. Such contacts and encounters are possible in one-to-one personal meetings, but I am also confident that I can engage with small groups through some programs.

I want to live by a very common truth. That is, I admit that everything is different: language, culture, customs, clothing, lifestyles, religion, race and so on. This difference offers hope. But I cannot reject the truth that all other truths come from one source and eventually return to the one root. For example, the stream in the area where I live flows from the nearby mountain. It provides my farmland and my house with water for drinking and general use. I depend on the water. Water flows and flows into the vast ocean. The sea is wide, but the water becomes as one. In the end, the water that flows in the rivers and eventually into the sea remains compatible as friends do. This analogy can be applied to our discussion of religion, life, faith and practice. The core of each religion has been fixed differently according to the culture and age, and each religion is practised in separately, but the ultimate reality that each religion seeks converges into one. Therefore, all religions are compatible with one another. Judaism, Buddhism, Confucianism, Christianity and folk religions live in the one water as close friends, but it is very important that they maintain their own traditions and way of life.

I think that bridging divisions through peace should be one of my life tasks. The type of bridge will vary according to the field. I will endeavour to build bridges in at least three ways: as an AVP activist, as a Quaker and as a member of Amnesty International. I hope to establish bridges and eliminate borders. In order to do so, I must experience other cultures, religions, people (races), civilisations and customs, either directly or indirectly, and find their core values and absorb them. It will be important to lead my life in the manner of those who always seek truth with an open mind.

Bibliography

Australia Yearly Meeting of Friends, *This We Can Say*, Canberra, 2003.
Brinton, H, *Friends for 300 Years*, Pennsylvania, 2002 (Korean translation).
Byun, S-H, *Encounter of Buddhism and Christianity* (Korea), Cheonan, 1997.
Chuang-tze, *Chuang-tze*, Chinese, Korean, English, German.
Fox, G, *The Journal of George Fox*, London, 2005 (Korean translation).
German Annual Meeting, *And What Can You Say?*, Bad Pyrmont, 2015.
Ham, SH, *An Anthology of Ham Sok Hon*, Seoul, 2001.
Ham, SH, *Queen of Suffering: A Spiritual History of Korea*, West Chester, PA, 1985.
Ham, SH, *Whole Works*, 1–20, (Korean) Seoul 1983–1987.
Hong, S-C, *Buddhism and Christianity* (Korean), Seoul, 1982.
Kim, S-H & K-S Lee, *Taoism and Christianity*, Seoul, 2003.
Kim, S-H & S-R Kim, *Christianism and Shamanism* (Korean), Seoul, 1998.
Küng, H & J Ching, *Christianity and Chinese Religions*, SCM Press, 1993 (Korean translation, 1994).
Lao-Tze, *Tao Te Ching* (King), Chinese, Korean, English, German.
Quakers in Britain, *Quaker Faith and Practice*, 3rd edn, London, 2005.
Smith, S, *Eastern Light: Awakening to Presence in Zen, Quakerism and Christianity*, Friends Bulletin Corporation, 2015.
Welch, HH, *Taoism: The Parting of the Way*, Beacon Press, 1957 (Korean translation, 1992).

www.ingramcontent.com/pod-product-compliance
Lightning Source LLC
LaVergne TN
LVHW051206080426
835508LV00021B/2844